MONCRIEF

To Rosemary

[signature]

MONCRIEF

My Journey to the NBA

Sidney Moncrief

WITH
Myra McLarey

August House Publishers, Inc.
LITTLE ROCK

Printed in the United States of America

10 9 8 7 6 5 4 3 2 1

LIBRARY OF CONGRESS CATALOGING-IN-PUBLICATION DATA

Moncrief, Sidney, 1957—
Moncrief : my journey to the NBA/
Sidney Moncrief with Myra McLarey.
—1st ed.   p.   cm.
ISBN 0-87483-113-X (alk. paper) : $14.95
1. Moncrief, Sidney, 1957—   .
2. Basketball players—United States—Biography.
3. Milwaukee Bucks (Basketball team)
I. McLarey, Myra, 1942—   . II. Title.
GV884.M58A3   1990
796.323'092—dc20 90-32704
[B] CIP

First Edition, 1990

Cover photograph courtesy Milwaukee Bucks
Book design by Communication Graphics
Typography by Heritage Publishing Co.
Project direction by Liz Parkhurst
Editorial assistance by Rod Lorenzen

This book is printed on archival-quality paper which meets the
guidelines for performance and durability of the Committee on
Production Guidelines for Book Longevity of the Council on Library Resources.

AUGUST HOUSE, INC.   PUBLISHERS   LITTLE ROCK

To two special people in my life:
my mother, Bernice Perkins,
and my wife, Debra

As with any work, no one does it alone. I'd like to thank some of the people and organizations who made this book possible: the *Arkansas Gazette,* the *Arkansas Democrat,* Rick Schaeffer of the Athletic Department at the University of Arkansas, Bill King Jr. of the Milwaukee Bucks organization, and Eddie Sutton.

My special appreciation goes to my husband, Steven, who suggested the idea to me; to Sidney's mom, Bernice Perkins, who let me rummage through all her scrapbooks and albums; to Cindra Coley, who cheerfully relayed a million phone messages; to Wally Hall and Bob Lutgen at the *Democrat,* who always took the extra step to help out; to Bob Ryan of the *Boston Globe;* to Bill Doshier, who kept the pictures he took while in high school tucked away in his basement; to Sue and Pee Wee, for still being my teammates; to Uncle Harold and Aunt Betty, for food, lodging and taxi service; to Martha Brown, for cheer; to Glenn Adelson, for the trips to the Garden; to my agent, Brian Zevnik, for his wit and unfailing support; and to Liz and Ted Parkhurst at August House, for believing in the project. Most of all I want to thank Sidney Moncrief for his time, his effort, and his grace.

—M.M.

INTRODUCTION

Everyone, it seems, has a Sidney Moncrief story. Maybe the setting is Lubbock: Texas Tech is ahead 65-64. Arkansas takes possession with twenty seconds remaining. As the *Arkansas Democrat*'s David McCollum tells it, "Everyone in Lubbock Municipal Coliseum knows the ball is going to Moncrief for the Hogs' last shot. Three men flock to him as he gets it with ten seconds left. Somehow, he finds that gap past the third defender and gets off a soft jumper. It glances off the front of the rim and falls through to give Arkansas a share of the Southwest Conference championship."

Or the setting is Houston, and Sidney hits a hot streak. Remember how he clapped his hands for the ball and, when he got it, made his leaping, twisting, turning moves for the basket? Was there any angle he didn't hit from that night?

Milwaukee fans have their share of stories, too. There's one about the playoff game the Bucks were losing to the Seattle Supersonics, at that time the defending NBA champs. Dave Meyers, the Bucks' veteran forward, fouls out with three minutes and thirty-nine seconds to play in overtime. Don Nelson puts in a short, skinny rookie—a guard at that. Moncrief, before a crowd of 14,050 and on a hostile court, gets a layup, a dunk and a bank shot before fans can say, "Sidney who?" Sidney scores all six of the Bucks' overtime points that night in their 114-112 victory.

Fans also like to recall the game on May 2, 1986, when the Bucks struggled against the 76ers in a playoff game. Sidney, now a veteran and often referred to as the 'heart and soul' of the Bucks, plays 37 minutes with a torn muscle in his left foot. He makes 16 points and gets 6 rebounds—one of them the biggest offensive rebound of the game. Anthony Cotton of the *Washington Post* described the play: "He somehow limped through a thicket of bodies to get the ball and put it back up for a score."

Some folks will tell you about Moncrief's wry sense of humor as they recall another game in that series with the 76ers. They'll tell you how Sidney played 38 minutes on a foot that he described as feeling like "someone pounding a nail in it." They remember how he plummeted to the floor after a layup and just lay there for a while. At half-time in the locker room, he shoved his foot into a chest of ice and joked: "I was trying to get sympathy from the crowd."

They remember the deciding game of the same series when Sidney scored 23 points, including a couple of "clutch" free-throws in the 113-112 win. The statistics pile up. And the stories go on.

But Sidney Moncrief stories aren't just about the thrill of watching him play, of watching his arms—quick as lightning—reach in and steal the ball, then send a perfect pass down the court to a teammate. Sidney Moncrief stories aren't just about an offensive style that was all his own, or the last-second shots that electrified the fans, or the brilliant defense that mystified his opponents.

Moncrief stories are set in North Carolina outside a dressing room where he stops to sign autographs for awestruck youngsters even though he has only five minutes to catch his plane. Or they're set in Fayetteville: Sidney is warming up for the last home game of his college career. He leaves the court, grabs his wife and mother by the arms and leads them to center court to a thunderous ovation. The stories are set in gyms where hundreds of kids, and former kids, look back and remember the encouragement and bits of wisdom Sidney gave them at basketball camp. The stories are set in schools where Moncrief shares with young people all he has learned—from growing up in a housing project—about the false promises of drugs, about the need for goals.

One story is set in Kenosha, Wisconsin, where people can tell you about the night Sidney played every minute of a game the Bucks won in overtime—he had 38 points, 8 rebounds and 12 assists—then drove the 35 miles to Kenosha to attend a church banquet.

Or the setting is before one of many civic groups across the country and Sidney has taken time from his demanding schedule to attend a fundraiser and talk about the needs of young people—about their need for education, about their need for hope. The list goes on, the miles stack up, as Sidney works his way through a calendar crowded with humanitarian projects.

My own particular story is set in South Paris, Maine. The year is 1979. It's a cold blustery day—as spring days are in Maine—and the sports pundits in the teachers' room are saying that Milwaukee has lost its marbles in picking Moncrief as its first-draft choice. They say, "Moncrief will sit on the bench a year or two, then he'll be gone." "His gimp knee will go out on him before the season is over." And knowing an Arkansan has one ear tuned to them as she reads the latest office memo, they intensify their pronouncements: "They'll have him for breakfast." "Why, that spindly thing, they'll chew him up and spit him out in no time flat." "Before the year is out, he'll find out what tough is and then he'll turn tail and head back to the hills of Arkansas where he belongs."

I start to tell them they are wrong. I start to tell them Sidney Moncrief will not only make it as a pro, he'll be one of the best. I start to tell them they don't know what Arkansas fans already know about his steely determination, his ability to lead, his ability to give his all every minute of the game, his solid—but never arrogant—confidence. I start to tell them that if they had watched the Texas A&M game the year before, if they had seen Sidney put an end to constant Aggie elbowing with some countermoves of his own, they'd know that Moncrief—never a bully himself—will not allow himself to be bullied. I start to tell them that folks back home know Moncrief is so much more than a ball player. They know that when he *does* head back to Arkansas where he belongs, he'll do so as a winner. I start to tell them they don't know butterbeans from black-eyed peas. But actually, they don't know either.

Instead, I throw the office memo in the wastebasket with all the others. I walk to the door, open it and, with my hand still on the doorknob, I say in as prophetic a tone as I can muster: "Just you wait."

Well, guys, care to take back what you said?

Everyone, it seems, has a Sidney Moncrief story—even Sidney. And this is his.

Myra McLarey
Cambridge, Massachusetts

NBA Statistics

SEASON	GAMES	POINTS	POINTS/ GAME	REBOUNDS	FIELD GOAL %	FREE THROW %
1979-80	77	654	8.5	338	46.8	79.5
1980-81	80	1122	14.0	406	54.1	80.4
1981-82	80	1581	19.8	534	52.3	81.7
1982-83	76	1712	22.5	437	52.7	82.6
1983-84	79	1654	20.9	528	49.8	84.8
1984-85	73	1585	21.7	391	48.3	82.8
1985-86	73	1471	20.2	334	48.9	85.9
1986-87	39	460	11.8	127	48.8	84.0
1987-88	56	603	10.8	180	48.9	83.7
1988-89	62	752	12.1	172	49.1	86.5
TOTALS	695	11594	16.7	3447	50.3	83.2

SOURCE: Milwaukee Bucks Organization

NCAA Statistics

SEASON	GAMES	POINTS	POINTS/ GAME	REBOUNDS	FIELD GOAL %	FREE THROW %
1975-76	28	354	12.6	213	66.5	72.7
1976-77	28	431	15.4	235	64.9	68.4
1977-78	36	621	17.3	278	59.0	79.3
1978-79	30	660	22.0	289	56.0	85.5
TOTALS	122	2066	16.9	1015	60.1	78.2

SOURCE: University of Arkansas Athletic Department

CHAPTER ONE

CHILDHOOD

CONTRARY TO WHAT SOME PEOPLE ASSUME, I wasn't born with a basketball in my hand. I started playing sandlot football when I was real young, but I probably didn't shoot my first basketball until the sixth grade. I was born in a segregated world, and I was poor. In a real sense, basketball was my way out of both segregation and poverty.

The house I was born in was in the John Barrow Addition in western Little Rock, a rural part of Pulaski County in those days. I was next to the youngest of seven kids, and we only had two bedrooms; we had to sleep three to a bed. We didn't have a bathroom or running water. We had to heat water to take a bath, and there would always be three of us to a tub. We didn't have much furniture at all. We did have an old black and white television but there weren't many shows for kids then so I didn't watch it much. Mostly, when I was little, I played outside in the yard with my brothers and sisters.

My mom and dad divorced when I was five years old. After that I saw my dad once every week or two, usually on Saturdays. We'd spend the day at his house. We'd cut the grass and do chores around the house. My father was a caring man who loved his kids, but he just never knew how to be a father. It was the same with a lot of black men: because of his history, my father wasn't confident enough to bear the responsibility that comes with having kids and being around them seven days a week. He was a great father for occasional visits. And at least I saw him enough to know that I had a father.

I think there's a lot to be said for having a mother and father in the household, but there's also a lot to be said for knowing where your father is and that he's close by if you need him. Recently, I was in downtown Little Rock at the annual Hoop-D-Do Tournament, and this little kid came over to me and said, "You know my mom!" He told me her name and I couldn't place her, so I said, "What's your daddy's name?" His response made me really sad; he said, "I don't know who my father is." That really hit me because we tend to take it for granted that everyone knows who his or her father is. In my case, that was enough—for me to know I had a father and that I could contact him when I wanted to.

Maybe my situation wasn't the norm, but I never understand the theories and articles I read about children from divorced homes being doomed to misery, because I never felt any trauma from my mother and father being separated. I felt its effects financially, because we had only one paycheck coming in. From an emotional standpoint, however, I didn't feel that I was any different from any other kid. I knew there was such turmoil when they were together that I cherished the peace and calm when they weren't. The biggest factor in my attitude towards my parents' divorce was the way my mom handled it: she didn't moan, or whine, or feel sorry for us—so neither did I.

Moncrief (right) in 1962 with sister Illene and brother Doyle (in high chair) in the house where he was born at 4124 Cobb Street in the John Barrow Addition of Little Rock. (courtesy Mrs. Bernice Perkins)

Moncrief (second from right) outside the Cobb Street home in 1962. In front are his cousins Ricky and Janette; middle, sister Emily and brother Doyle; and back right, brother George. (courtesy Mrs. Bernice Perkins)

My mom didn't remarry until I was fourteen, so she had the sole responsibility of supporting us for most of my childhood. She cleaned the rooms at Howard Johnson's—working long, hard hours and making less than fifty dollars a week. Since that had to take care of herself and seven kids, she never had the money—or the time—to take us to stores, or movies, or parks. I never experienced those kinds of things. We only left the house to go to school and to church.

In one sense, I saw my mom as a beaten-down woman, working all the time. She didn't have much time to be happy. She didn't have much time to spend with her kids. She pretty much was caught up in waking up, fixing breakfast, going to work, coming home, getting something on the table to eat, and going to sleep—repeating that process over and over again. So we never really saw any happiness on her face. We just saw a lot of strain from having to care for all of us by herself.

I watched my mom struggle, but like most kids, I thought the only thing that was

Moncrief (right) in 1966 with his brother George and niece Jennifer. In background is the family home at #8 Hollingsworth in East End Housing Project. (courtesy Mrs. Bernice Perkins)

really important was what *I* was doing. The fact that she had a job at minimum wage and was trying to raise all of us kids, the fact that she worked around the clock, the fact that she never had a moment to herself—none of that was important. What *was* important was having a bicycle that I'd seen and wanted (and never did get)—things like that.

Still, I consider my childhood very happy. I enjoyed life. I didn't know how poor and deprived we were because everyone around us was poor too. It was just a part of our lives. So I just carried on my childhood. It wasn't until later that I could look back and appreciate my mom's struggle.

Now I realize my mom was a strong and determined person. She set a great example by owning up to her responsibilities. She didn't run away from them; she didn't make excuses; she just did what she had to do. And she did it the honest way. We incorporated her values into our lives and became better people. The discipline was certainly there. She didn't allow us to show disrespect to other people. And most of all, she didn't allow us to show her disrespect. If she caught us doing wrong, she punished us; if we did right—that's what we were expected to do. We weren't bribed or rewarded for it.

She also insisted that we pull our weight around the house. From the time we were very small, we had chores to do. Most of the boys in our neighborhood who had sisters didn't have to do much; the girls did everything. But in our household, we rotated doing dishes, mopping the floor, ironing the clothes ... There were no chores that were girls' chores or boys' chores, except for sewing, and even then if my mom was too tired and I needed a botton sewed on, I'd have to do it. We all worked very hard.

But with my mom gone so much, I still had lots of time to kill, lots of time to get in trouble.

Moncrief bids his mother farewell at the Little Rock Airport. (photo by Steve Keesee, courtesy Arkansas Gazette)

CHAPTER TWO

YOUTH

Moncrief creates a memory for kids at hoop camp. (Photo by Mark Baldwin, courtesy Arkansas Democrat)

THE STREET I LIVED ON WHEN I WAS VERY young was all black, but white families lived nearby. Very early on I learned about racism. It was like something in the air. If you were black, you didn't walk through a white neighborhood without sensing the hostility. And if you were white, you were met with that same hostility if you walked in the black neighborhood. It worked both ways.

I can recall running into some white children occasionally when I was seven or so. They'd call us niggers and we'd call them peckerwoods. We didn't even know each other but we had heard others called that. We tossed the word nigger around a lot in the black community—calling each other that without thinking of the ramifications, without thinking what it meant.

That same year, we moved to Little Rock's East End Housing Project. After that, we were totally segregated. We did not come in contact with whites at all, except for rare trips downtown. And with Momma gone all the time, I found plenty of things to get into as I got older. I had so many fights I couldn't count them. I was skinny so I got beat up a lot, but I beat up plenty of my friends too. I was lucky I never got seriously injured. I got plenty of busted lips and black eyes, though.

I remember one fight I had with my friend Robert (we called him Pig). We were best friends, but we always fought. It seemed like we fought once a day. This particular day there were four or five guys standing around watching. They were mostly Robert's friends as I hadn't lived there in the projects very long. Robert usually beat me, but this day I started getting the best of him for once. I was actually winning. We didn't always fight that clean so he reached down and picked up a stick; I picked up a tire strip. That's the first time I remember running, but I can tell you I ran.

Then another time when I was in junior high, I had a fight with a guy whose name I've forgotten. We were fighting and I was winning. He picked up a stick; I picked up a stick. We were going round and round in a circle, swinging our sticks. Then he stopped and said, "Okay, you put down your stick and I'll put down mine." That seemed like a good idea to me, so I did. But he didn't put his down—he headed towards me. I ran that time too. I never did believe a thing he said after that.

Later, we started stealing. We stole every chance we got. Sometimes, we went to the airport, which was nearby, to see if we could pick anything up. If anybody left their car windows open, we'd reach in and get whatever had been left on the seats. But we didn't break into any cars.

Mostly we stole from the grocery store in our neighborhood—a dinky little store owned by Mr. Berry. Everything in it must have been at least two years old since the inventory didn't turn very much—it just kind of sat there gathering dust. I stole candy bars every day. Baby Ruths were my favorite.

One morning, Mr. Berry was there by himself when we dropped in on our way to school—even though we were already late. We saw some money sitting on his cash register. We decided one of us would tell Mr. Berry he wanted something in the case to get his attention away from the cash register; then one of us would take the money. There were four of us. I was the one who said, "I want that candy bar. No, not that one, that one"—then I'd change my mind—"No, I think I want this one." While I had Mr. Berry trying to find the right candy bar, one of the guys reached over and took the money. The loot came to four or five dollars of quarters, nickels, and dimes. It was the only time I ever took money. It could have been the beginning of a life of crime for me.

My stealing didn't have anything to do with drugs. It had to do with boredom and poverty—and with the fact that everyone else was doing it. I knew what I was doing was wrong, but at first I didn't consider that I had the option of not doing it.

I didn't have a time when I said, "Now, I'll stop stealing." But I stopped, I think, because of a choice my mother made. No matter how tired she was, she saw to it that we went to church every Sunday morning. Getting ready for church could be a real drag.

We took our once-a-week bath on Saturday night—Doyle, George and I would have to share the tub. We didn't have to worry about what to wear because we had only one set of church clothes. For me, breakfast—not church—was the highlight of Sunday; we'd have a huge breakfast of rice, biscuits, bacon and eggs. Then it was off to church. It wasn't my favorite place to be, but once I got there, it wasn't usually so bad.

Without a doubt, being raised in a Christian home and going to church influenced me—not so much when I was a kid, but as I got older. It gave me a foundation to reach back and draw upon. I knew what was right and good, and I knew I would be punished if I got caught doing wrong. So when I was stealing, it was always

lurking in the back of my mind: "This isn't really right."

Eventually that moral pressure helped me make better choices. A lot of kids I knew hadn't been forced to go to church and learn about Christ, and they didn't have anything else to draw upon later in life. Consequently, many of them ended up in prison at Cummings or Tucker; I have a number of friends who did. They're still friends, but they haven't found their way.

My early education had nothing to do with "dear old golden school days." I had some good times, but I had some very bad times. I was an average student. I had the ability to learn, but I also had the ability to talk, and to be disruptive,

Moncrief and his fellow Razorbacks became role models for many Arkansas youth. (Photo by Pat Patterson, courtesy Arkansas Gazette)

Moncrief credits his mother with keeping his family together. (Photo by Steve Keesee, courtesy Arkansas Gazette)

and to fight. I felt that old strap and paddle several times in school. I wasn't usually stupid enough to get paddled over and over for the same things, but I got paddled for a variety of things over the course of time. I never felt that the teachers doing the paddling really cared about me; they cared about the classroom, and order, but not about me. I'm sad to say I had plenty of teachers that gave me no sense that they were there to serve my best interest, to lead me and to help me learn. I could always tell a difference

between a teacher who was teaching the subject, and a teacher who was teaching the student.

But I also had teachers who cared about me. And that was important. Certain people had a big effect on me; my first-grade teacher, Mrs. Lewis, was one of those. I'm not sure her teaching methods were the best, but it was my first experience at being confined and working within a system. She was able to control the classroom not because she was bigger—or stronger—but because she had confidence in herself.

I remember one particular day of first grade like it was yesterday. That was the day someone walked into the classroom and told Mrs. Lewis that President Kennedy had been shot and killed. Mrs. Lewis started crying. I remember that vividly. I didn't understand much about it, but I knew something awful had happened if Mrs. Lewis was crying about it.

Ironically, the teacher I remember most wasn't a classroom teacher but a Scout leader. When I was ten, the Salvation Army formed a Cub Scout pack and recruited a group of us kids in east Little Rock. What sold us on joining was the uniform. We had to pay one dollar for a used Scout uniform. They were too short—the sleeves on mine came just below my elbows. They were faded. Some of them were patched. But we didn't care. It was a uniform, and it was neat.

We all joined the Cub Scouts, and in a year or so we got to be Boy Scouts. Our troop leader was a white guy from Boston named Dave Shaeffer. That was my first real contact with a white person, and it was a positive one. After my mom remarried and we moved, Mr. Shaeffer would drive all the way to our house to take my brother and me back to east Little Rock for the meetings and then he'd drive us home. He eventually left, and I've wondered what happened to him. He probably doesn't know he played such an important role in my childhood.

Being in Scouts was the first time any of us had been involved in any organized activity that offered a learning atmosphere. We met once a week at the Salvation Army building. We learned how to tie knots, how to build fires and other survival skills. We went on trips to Camp Quapaw. And we were constantly hearing, "A Boy Scout is courteous, kind, obedient, cheerful ..." We were hearing it—and believing it. We still got into trouble, but we got into much less trouble than we would have if we hadn't been in Boy Scouts. I was too busy to have stealing on my mind. I had other things to do, things that were good for me, things that made me feel good about myself.

When my mom remarried, we moved out of the projects to a house on Gaines Street. This also helped keep me out of trouble. For one thing, I wasn't always with friends who were getting in trouble. Another thing that helped keep me out of trouble, believe it or not, was a garden.

My mom and stepfather had a garden plot out in the country, around Sweet Home. It was enormous—it must have been about an acre. How I dreaded working in that garden! We planted in March, April and May. We'd till the soil to get it ready. Then we'd rake it and plant it. The best time was in August and September when we picked and then ate what we had grown. But between planting and harvesting, we had to go out in the sweltering sun to pull the weeds and push the dirt up around the plants. I'd see all my friends going off to play basketball and there we'd be, going off to the garden—which didn't make me very happy.

A lot of times, I'd go to the garden, come back about seven and then go to the community center and shoot basketball until nine or so. I did miss out on a lot of fun, but I didn't have as much time to get into trouble, and I learned a lot. For one thing, I learned keeping a garden is hard work!

My first paying job, during the summers in high school, was hard work too. My uncle was a contractor, and he hired my brother George and me to paint houses at fifty cents an hour. We didn't think that was enough, so we decided to go on strike to get one dollar an hour. He came to pick us up one Monday morning and George and I were sitting on the steps but we didn't budge. We told him we weren't going to work until we got more money. That lasted several days, maybe even a week, before he gave in and we went back to work.

Although working helped keep me out of trouble, I can't say I didn't do stupid things. I can't say I didn't try drugs. I attended Dunbar and Booker junior high schools at the end of the 1960s, and drugs were already on the scene. Cocaine was not big back then, but LSD and heroin were—and marijuana was everywhere. Everyday, somebody at school or on the street would have some drugs to offer. I tried marijuana because I was curious—and because my friends were doing it.

Then it dawned on me that the only thing drugs did for me was make me accepted by the people on drugs. They didn't improve anything I was doing. They didn't make me smarter, or faster. They didn't make me grow stronger, or taller. I just didn't see any benefit in doing drugs.

Some people say drugs make them feel better, but they didn't make me feel better. They made me feel out of control, and out of touch with myself. By the time I was in high school, some of my friends were shooting up a lot. But I didn't involve myself with them when they were messing with drugs, even though we were still friends. I had already figured out that drugs make a lot of promises

Children at Arkansas School for the Deaf honor the man who has been an inspiration to young people throughout the country.

they don't keep.

Still, it's not that hard to understand why people try them. We live in a society that prepares us to have a mindset for drugs. Television is always telling us to take a drug: if you have a headache, take a drug; if you have a stomachache, take a drug; if you can't sleep, take a drug. That kind of thinking makes it easier for people to accept and start using illegal drugs.

Poverty breeds a hopelessness which can also lead to drugs. Recently, I went by the project where I grew up. I was shocked. In my memory at least, it had been a place where people had a sense of pride—in how their houses looked, and how their yards looked. We kept them neat and clean, and we felt the housing authority took pride in the projects.

Not so, today. The grass is high, and everything looks run down. I didn't expect that. It is a real sign of hopelessness. It's difficult on a young person when he is living in that environment because the parents tend to impose their hopelessness on the child. Their attitude is, "I didn't make it and the world is getting worse, so you're not going to make it either." Parents who've lost hope don't say to their children, "You could become a good carpenter," or "You sure can draw, you could become an artist."

I liked to draw when I was a kid. I didn't create scenes; I just tried to draw what I saw. But we didn't have art in school then, and no one encouraged me to do it. By the time I got to junior high, I had lost interest. If I had gotten encouragement when I was in the third grade, I might have kept on drawing.

Unfortunately, we don't take the time to develop those talents a kid has, unless he's an athlete. We're much quicker to say, "Gosh, did you see my kid dribble that ball?" than we are to say, "Have you seen the table my kid built?" There are many other kinds of talent that are just as valuable—or more valuable—to our society than athletic talent. My talent just happened to be basketball. But I didn't know that for a long time.

CHAPTER THREE

HIGH SCHOOL

SINCE WE DIDN'T HAVE ANY BASKETBALL courts in the project, a friend's backyard was the only place I had to play until I got to junior high. I wasn't that good when I first started playing, but I liked it because it was something I could play with others, and something I could do by myself. I liked the fact that I could get better by playing by myself. I remember going out and working on layups, and telling myself, "I *am* going to get to a point where I can make this layup every time." I presented myself with those kinds of challenges—not because I wanted to

(*Photo by Steve Keesee, courtesy Arkansas Gazette*)

be on the main team, or because I wanted to be a star or a professional player, but because I just wanted to get better than I was.

I played my first official game when I was in junior high school. I was on the C team because I wasn't good enough to be on the A or B team. I was pretty tall—in the neighborhood they called me Slim—but I was skinny and weak.

I didn't make the main team until I was in the ninth grade. It didn't really bother me because I knew there were guys who were better players, but it motivated me to get better. So I worked as hard as I could and then I didn't worry about what team I was on.

(Frankly, I worried more about my hair not growing very long. Back then, the in thing was to have a big Afro, and my hair would only get to a certain point and then stop. I was embarrassed that it wouldn't grow longer because I wanted a big Afro pretty bad.)

I understood why I was on the bench, but I did want the chance to prove myself on the court. I think everybody who sits on the bench dreams of going into a game and doing something spectacular—like getting that crucial rebound, or intercepting a pass, or making that last-second shot to win the game—but it doesn't always work out that way. When I did get a chance to play, I wasn't always that great—to say the least.

One time when Coach Kelly, the assistant coach, put me in the game, I got the ball and was dribbling down the court. I had my head down because I was watching that ball for all it was worth, so I didn't see my teammate open under the basket, yelling for the ball. I just kept dribbling down the court and took a layup that I had practiced over and over and over. I missed.

Coach Kelly, whose anger was written all over his face, called time-out. He pulled me aside and hollered, "Didn't you see he was open?"

I said, "No, Coach."

Then he hit me in the chest with the back of his hand. That was an embarrassing moment for me. To this day, my best friend

As a senior, Moncrief was named to seven different high school All-American teams. (courtesy Mrs. Bernice Perkins)

teases me about it. I can laugh about it now, but at the time it was not one bit funny. It could have broken me, but I had grown up in a tough neighborhood and had toughened up myself. Tough or not, it shook me up, and I was no good the rest of the game.

Still, the standards Coach Kelly sometimes set had something to do with my staying out of trouble. Once in the eighth grade, I did something really stupid. I was smoking a cigarette in the locker room when we were getting ready to leave on the bus—a very small van. Coach Kelly came in and caught me, and he made me stay behind. "Moncrief," he said, "we wouldn't take you on this trip if we had a Greyhound bus."

I still did some questionable things. But the coach's standards probably kept me from doing more. Looking back, I realize playing basketball was a way of getting out my aggression, but I didn't know it then.

I made All-City and All-Tournament in the ninth grade. That was the first award of any kind I had ever received. It gave me a sense of satisfaction, but not as much as I had thought it would. From that time on, awards were important—but not *that* important. I like to receive them, but my satisfaction comes from knowing I've done a good job.

After I entered high school at Little Rock Hall, I made the main team. By my senior year, I was considered one of the best players in the state. That's when I started to realize I *was* a good player; during the summer between my junior and senior years I realized playing in college was a possibility. I had spent grades nine, ten, and eleven not doing my homework; I had always done just enough to get by, even though I knew that I could do better. Needless to say, my grade point had deteriorated.

For the first time, I had an ambition: I wanted to be a coach. And I was facing a major obstacle. I had a 1.85 average, and I had to have a 2.0 to get an athletic scholarship at a major college. The situation did not look promising.

In 1977-79, Moncrief led the Hogs to 102 wins and three Southwest Conference championships. (Courtesy University of Arkansas Athletic Department)

That's when Coach Elders stepped in. Oliver Elders was, and is, quite a man. Since he had a family, he didn't have time to take us places like Coach Ripley, his assistant, did. But his influence on us was powerful: he wanted us to excel in the classroom as well as on the court. He also emphasized the importance of respecting other people. He insisted on things like taking off our hats when we we entered the building, saying "yes, ma'am" and "yes, sir," letting older people go first. He insisted that we dress well when we went to our games. We didn't have to wear ties, but we had to wear a clean dress shirt, pressed slacks and clean shoes. He demanded things that have served me well.

Coach Elders gave me quite a talking to—about my grades and about my future. He told me I had the talent to play college basketball, but if I wanted to make it I'd better get as serious about my studies as I was about the sport. I figured he was right, so I devoted my senior year to getting my grades up. Disciplining myself to study was a new experience for me, but I was leaving

high school with a goal—to be a coach. And to do that, I had to have a college degree—so study I did.

I learned more in high school than how to play basketball and how to study; I learned how to live in an integrated world. Even though I was born the year and the month of Little Rock's Central High School crisis—September, 1957—I spent my childhood in a segregated world and in segregated schools. We were too poor to even

(Photo courtesy Arkansas Democrat)

33

In high school, Moncrief wasn't always the most graceful, but he got the job done. (courtesy Mrs. Bernice Perkins)

think about eating at lunch counters at the dime stores—Momma never took us to those stores. Before high school, the one thing that forced me to confront what I was otherwise sheltered from was some reading I did on my own. *Black Boy, Native Son, Go Tell it on the Mountain*—those books let me know what the civil rights struggle was all about. Richard Wright and James Baldwin—in their books—

put racism right on the table and said to me, "Hey, this is real. These are real events that happen in people's lives and it's probably going to happen in your life." Reading those books helped prepare me to face those attitudes that were—and are—there.

When I entered Hall, black students hung out with black students, and whites hung out with whites. I saw my share of

Somehow he always seemed to find a way to reach over the arms of his opponent. (Photo by Steve Keesee, courtesy Arkansas Gazette)

In 1975, sportswriter Wadie Moore foreshadowed what lay ahead for the Hall High senior: "One day, the name of Sidney Moncrief will find its rightful place in this state's basketball history. You'll remember him." (courtesy Mrs. Bernice Perkins)

fights. Some black guys would band together and beat up a white kid in the bathrooms. And vice versa. I didn't get into those fights because I knew I'd get kicked off the team if I did. The fights were mainly the result of distrust, fear, and of not knowing each other. And they could be brutal.

Still, integration was the best thing that could have happened to me. For the first time, I was interacting with whites. It helped me to understand them better, and it helped me learn how to get along with them. It gave me a chance to get past what my parents said about whites. And it gave white kids a chance to get over what their parents said about us.

Integration also presented me with a challenge. Growing up in a separate world, I had always felt like a normal kid. Once I started attending school with whites and saw they had better clothes, more money, nicer cars, and in many cases, a stronger educational background, it was hard not to develop feelings of inferiority.

I saw that black kids used to making straight A's were no longer making A's. Some of them were so devastated by that they retreated into a shell. But then I saw how many of the black kids saw being in a harder school as a challenge and rose to the occasion. I began to see it wasn't a case of being superior or inferior, but a case of

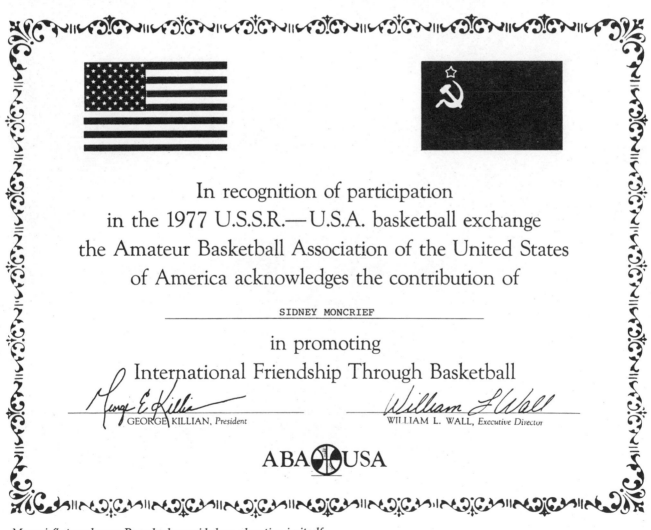

In recognition of participation
in the 1977 U.S.S.R.—U.S.A. basketball exchange
the Amateur Basketball Association of the United States
of America acknowledges the contribution of

SIDNEY MONCRIEF

in promoting
International Friendship Through Basketball

GEORGE KILLIAN, *President*

WILLIAM L. WALL, *Executive Director*

ABA◯USA

Moncrief's travels as a Razorback provided an education in itself.

having the opportunity, and of taking advantage of that opportunity.

And I was motivated to take advantage of that opportunity, so I decided to stay busy doing things that helped keep me out of trouble. Basketball and church were two of those things. And having the goal of going to college was another.

In the end, it all boils down to an individual choice. I could have chosen to keep stealing, to keep taking drugs, and to keep on slacking off on my homeowork. Some of the kids I grew up with continued stealing, and then they went to robbing—which just leads to trouble.

It helped that I had a girlfriend whose head was on straight. I've known my wife, Debra, since I was in the third grade and she was in second. We lived fairly close—I was on the hill and she was down below—but we ran with a different set of friends. We started dating my senior year.

I'll never forget our first date. I was taking her to see *The Horror of the Wax Museum*. I'd seen the previews and it looked good and scary.

We went to the John Miller Quartet on University and entered the movie theater. We were a little late, so we had missed all the credits and the movie was just getting started. We no sooner sat down when this lady in the film started taking off all her

Oliver Elders, Moncrief's high school basketball coach, wishes him well after Moncrief returns to his high school gym to announce his retirement. (Photo by Steve Keesee, courtesy Arkansas Gazette)

clothes. Then she and the man started
making love ...

We had gone into the wrong theater.
Needless to say, that was an awkward
situation. We were both thinking: "What *is*
this!" I think I was the one who suggested
that we must be in the wrong movie theater.
She agreed. That was very embarrassing—
especially since it was our first date. It didn't
help much that the right movie—the one I
had bragged about being so scary—was
terrible and not the least bit frightening. As
usual, they had shown all the good parts on
the previews.

In spite of the disastrous first date,
Debra agreed to go out with me again. And
again. We got married before my senior year
in college. I married the right girl. That's a
big key to life. She was a stabilizing
influence, and she certainly agreed with
Coach that I needed to study more.

And my studying did pay off. I got my
grade point up, and scholarship offers began
to pour in.

CHAPTER FOUR

COLLEGE

"Sidney Moncrief is the most beloved athlete in the history of Arkansas."—Jaime Diaz, Sports Illustrated (Photo by Pat Patterson, courtesy Arkansas Gazette)

LSU, ARKANSAS, AND ARKANSAS STATE recruited me the heaviest. I was recruited by other schools, but I narrowed it down to those three very quickly. I did visit the University of Minnesota in September and it was about thirty degrees and snowing. That's when I decided not to go very far from home.

I found LSU appealing. The arena was very nice, and I liked the size of the school. Baton Rouge had an atmosphere similar to that of Little Rock, the campus was beautiful—and they were in a good basketball conference.

I was even more tempted to go to Arkansas State than to LSU. I'd worked in ASU's basketball camp and had a good relationship with the coaching staff— especially John Rose and Bill Tyler.

Arkansas, however, had a new coach—Eddie Sutton. He was making promises about the type of basketball he would play—fundamentally sound, aggressive both on defense and offense, and with an emphasis on teamwork. In his first year alone—my senior year at Hall—he was already making good things happen.

Arkansas didn't offer me any more than LSU or Arkansas State; all three of those schools recruited me clean. I did get some hints from an out-of-state school that I would get some good clothes and be well taken care of, but they only hinted. I think college athletic programs try to buy players only when they see they can. Even as a high school student, I would have recognized the offer of a car and spending money as wrong. That's not to say I wouldn't have found it flattering or that it would have been easy to turn down.

Largely because of Eddie Sutton, I decided to go to the University of Arkansas. I felt his program would go farther than that of any other Arkansas school, and I saw a chance to be a part of an Arkansas program that would bring nationwide recognition to the state. In the past, most of the better players had left the state to play. I wanted to be on a team that showed people that guys from Arkansas

could play with the best, and win.

Coach Ripley, Coach Elders' assistant at Hall, had expanded my world by taking us to Memphis, Dallas and other places to watch college and NBA ball. He took me to the second pro game I ever saw, featuring the New Jersey Nets and the Memphis Tams. That's the first time I saw Dr. J play. Watching him play was more exciting than I can say. I never in my wildest dreams imagined I'd be playing on the same court with him someday.

Those trips were important experiences for me. We got a chance to see how well the game could be played; and, in leaving the state, we got a feeling of the attitudes people

Moncrief respected Eddie Sutton and always listened to his instructions. (courtesy Arkansas Democrat)

(Photo by Gary Speed, courtesy Arkansas Gazette)

had about Arkansas—that we were inferior, that we were country bumpkins. So it was a matter of pride that I could be part of a college team that showed the world kids from Arkansas could compete with the best.

I think we did show them that. We had good people on the squad, and Coach Sutton turned us into a good team—and that's what we were, a team. The concept of the Triplets—Ron Brewer, Marvin Delph and me—was more of a media hype than anything else. The three of us really didn't pay much attention to it; it didn't dawn on me how the three of us had jelled until we had finished playing together. When we were playing, I didn't think of the three of us as a unit. We were a twelve-man team.

Marvin and Ron and I were very lucky to be part of a team that didn't have enormous egos. Obviously when you have twelve people together, you're going to have people who don't particularly like each other; I have that now in my business. But that's not important when you have a job to do. What's important is that you do what you should to help the team win. I think most of the players had the attitude, *We'll put aside any feelings that interfere with our playing. Right now, we need to go out, play good basketball, and win.*

I certainly had no idea that I was part of a "legend" in Arkansas basketball history— no idea at all—until four or five years later. I just knew we had a good team, that we went to the final four, that we had done extremely well—that was it.

Coach Sutton was the perfect college coach for me. He was a hard coach— very demanding, very firm, but he was also very fair. He was a perfect motivator not only from an athletic standpoint, but from an academic and public relations standpoint as well. He wanted each of us to be the best basketball player we could be, but he also wanted us to be prepared for life.

After Debra and my mother, Eddie Sutton has probably had more influence on me than anyone. He came along at what I

(Photo by Steve Keesee, courtesy Arkansas Gazette)

think is the most crucial age in a person's life. In junior high and high school, you have your family, the influence of a father or mother, brothers, sisters, and friends. I had left my family to go off to college, and Coach Sutton and the assistant coaches became my parents in a sense.

Some college coaches want their players to just play ball and other than that do what they please. When those players graduate—*if* they graduate—and go on their own, they're going to have the same nonchalant attitude.

(Photo by Steve Keesee, courtesy Arkansas Gazette)

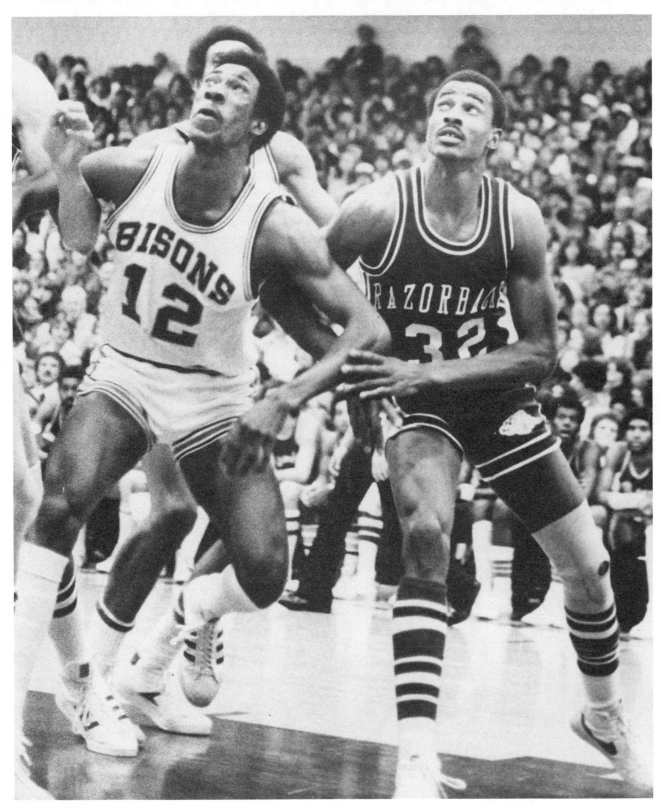

(courtesy Arkansas Democrat)

They're not going to be able to focus and be disciplined.

But Coach Sutton taught us how to excel in all walks of life. We worked very hard on the basketball court. We had to be on time. We had to work as a team. We had to be respectful to and of each other. He insisted on sportsmanship, ethical behavior, and integrity. He insisted that we get along with others on the team, and that we listen to him and to each other. Those are factors which are necessary to be productive in life, not just on the ball court.

Coach Sutton also had strong assistant coaches, whom we knew we could go to if

we had any kind of personal problem. Somehow it was a little intimidating to talk to the head coach about small but important matters. I think he understood that, so he made sure his assistant coaches were the kind of people the players could go to. The primary assistant coaches when I was there were Pat Foster and Gene Keady. They shared Coach Sutton's philosophies about basketball, education and moral behavior, so we got immersed in his philosophy wherever we turned.

Likewise, Coach Sutton recruited the kind of players that felt comfortable talking with each other about problems. In

Moncrief (fifth from right) adjusted to the grueling schedule of college play—but he never learned to like the cold. (courtesy University of Arkansas Athletic Department)

As a kid, Moncrief worked for hours on layups, telling himself, "I am going to get to a point where I can make this layup every time." (Photo by James Allison, courtesy Arkansas Democrat)

Moncrief's heads-up play prompted Wadie Moore to write: "Moncrief has that sixth sense that enables him to take charge in many games." (Photo courtesy Arkansas Democrat)

recruiting, he looked at the player as the person he was, as well as the kind of basketball he played. With very few exceptions, he recruited only those who would fit in with the other players as a person and who would fit in to the university as a student.

Needless to say, I was saddened by the troubles Coach Sutton encountered later as head coach at the University of Kentucky. He never even hinted at any

Baylor falls prey to Eddie Sutton's defense—spearheaded by Moncrief—and Arkansas is on its way to a 26-2 1978 season. (Photo by Gary Speed, courtesy Arkansas Gazette)

(Photo by Gary Speed, courtesy Arkansas Gazette)

*M*arch 3, 1979: The Razorbacks and Longhorns battle it out in Houston in the Southwest Conference Post-Season Classic. The game has more the marks of the Battle of the Bulge than a Texas shoot-out. By turns each team advances, is pushed back, then advances again. It is a game of control, of holding on to what you have—a game where each team sweats blood for a point. It is a war of nerves.

Tyrone Branyan, the Longhorns' 6'7" forward, sharpens his aims, finds his target and hits seven straight points to tie the Hogs 26-26 with 9:08 left on the clock.

Eddie Sutton calls time-out and tells Moncrief it's time for him to take over the game. When play resumes, Moncrief is now the one guarding Branyan with the tenacity of a pit bull. Sidney also hits two straight twisters to help Arkansas regain the lead.

With 48 seconds left, Branyan narrows the UA lead to 37-36. The Longhorns, tasting victory, trap Alan Zahn at mid-court; John Danks ties him up.

The ball is tipped toward the Arkansas goal but a Longhorn has the step on the ball. Then, seemingly out of nowhere, U.S. Reed charges in and grabs the ball at the baseline. "From where I was, I didn't think there was any way U.S. would get to it, but he just did it," Sidney will say later. Reed feeds it to Moncrief, who gently lays the ball in the basket—assuring victory for the Razorbacks. Moncrief is named the tournament's Most Valuable Player. And Arkansas is bound for the NCAA playoffs.

Moncrief looks to pass against Texas A&M. (Photo by Steve Keesee, courtesy Arkansas Gazette)

impropriety with me.

I can't say that during my time in Arkansas I wasn't offered anything extra. I can't say that occasionally an alumnus or overzealous fan didn't walk up to me after a game and put a hundred-dollar bill in my hand when he shook it.

But I sure didn't get anything extra from the coaching staff. Once I got picked up for speeding in Ozark, Arkansas, and I got a fifty-five dollar speeding ticket. I told Coach Sutton about it, thinking he'd probably help me out. But he told me there was nothing he

could do, his hands were tied. So I took five dollars a month out of my laundry money to pay it off.

I do think the rules concerning compensation of college athletes are too strict. We were expected to survive for four years off a scholarship that paid tuition, books, room and board and eighteen dollars a month laundry money. We couldn't keep up our practice schedule and studies and work any kind of a job, except in the summer. My mom worked as hard as she could, but she couldn't afford to send me money, even

Moncrief (bottom left) and his teammates celebrate winning the 1977 Southwest Conference championship. (courtesy University of Arkansas Athletic Department)

Moncrief and teammates claim another victory. (Photo by Gary Speed, courtesy Arkansas Gazette)

though she sometimes did.

When rules are too strict, people are encouraged to break them. I mean, when you can't fly a kid home from a road game to see his dying grandmother, something isn't fair.

It seems to me, if college programs had more reasonable compensation across the board—we're not talking extravagance, just the basics, like a much-needed coat or pair of shoes—then they could say no to the

On to the NCAA: Sutton hugs Moncrief after the Hogs' win over the University of Louisville. (Photo by Steve Keesee, courtesy Arkansas Gazette)

Moncrief demonstrates one of the moves that made him the first recipient of the Southwest Conference Most Valuable Player Award. (Photo by James Allison, courtesy Arkansas Democrat)

(Photo by Gary Speed, courtesy Arkansas Gazette)

Fans bid farewell to Moncrief before his last game in Barnhill Arena. (courtesy University of Arkansas Athletic Department)

Larry Bird recalls being guarded by Moncrief in the 1979 playoff game in the Midwest finals

Moncrief, guarded by Larry Bird, scores the basket that puts Arkansas ahead 47-45 with 16:30 left in the game during the 1979 NCAA playoffs. (Indiana State won the game by one point.) (Photo by Steve Keesee, courtesy Arkansas Gazette)

*E*ven after all these years, every time I see Sidney I think most about the college game we played. I had never even heard of him. Coach told us we'd better pay attention to this guy because he'd be running on us, dunking on us, dogging us every minute of the game.

I thought Coach was building him up too much. I thought, how in the heck can this guy be good and we've never heard of him? But he **was** that good, and the last few minutes of the game when he guarded me he was all over me. I compare that experience with being guarded by Michael Cooper now.

Sidney could do everything. He was a lot stronger than he looked. He could post low; he had good sharp cuts in terms of jump shooting. He had perfect form—you'd want a kid to model jump shots after his.

But most of all, the amazing thing about Sidney was his grasp of the game. He knew what to do and when to do it.

athletes' getting anything else and expect most athletes to comply. As it is, it's very difficult to get by on what's offered.

College athletics is a big business; the athlete, however, is not compensated for it other than by a scholarship. Because there are unfair demands on his time, he misses out on an opportunity to get involved in the other activities his university has to offer. Ideally, a student should be involved in a variety of pursuits in order to expand his education. But a student who has to practice three hours a day, who has to spend a lot of time on the road does not have that choice.

I've read about coaches who make players wake up at five or six in the morning to practice basketball—as a type of discipline. We didn't have to do that, but it was very common not to be able to go home for breaks, for Thanksgiving, or for Christmas. I dreaded not going home for the holidays. It's unfair to always take those experiences away from any student. It's unfair to take away time from his studies, his family and his university life.

As it is now, it smacks of a plantation system. The university goes for the bucks— the television revenues, especially—and demands everything of the athlete. In turn the athlete gets room, board and tuition, but he doesn't get time to be a part of anything else.

Now I'll admit the athlete has the opportunity to get an education out of the deal. That is a fair exchange. Ultimately, the individual has the choice of whether to use the system or let the system use him—or her. But let's not forget that we're talking about seventeen-, eighteen-, nineteen-year-old kids: they don't have good study habits; they don't know what they want out of life; some of them have good moral support from home and some don't. Unless they get very good guidance, then they don't avail themselves of the opportunity to get something out of the deal; they end up being used.

Unless the athlete gets a quality education, or unless he's one of the lucky ones who make it to the pros, he's left out on the vine to wilt and die. It should be made

absolutely clear to everyone that getting an education is the first priority for both the athlete and the school.

This is essentially what Coach Sutton told me. The way he put it to me was, "I can't offer you anything but a chance to get a college education and a chance to play in a good program." To my knowledge, Eddie Sutton ran a clean program.

Our schedule at the university was grueling. As far as schedules are concerned, college athletics is as difficult as the pros. During pre-season we'd go to class all or most of the morning. My classes usually began about 7:30 and I'd be done between noon and 1:30. Then I'd usually take a nap or study, and by 3:00 or 3:30, we'd be on the court. Practice ran until 5:30 or 6:00; after dinner, the freshmen and those who were having problems with a class would have study hall for an hour.

Our course requirements were monitored, and in my entire four years there, I didn't take any course that wasn't a requirement for graduation or an accepted elective. The coaches wanted us to stay on track for our degree. Through the athletic director's office, they received all of our grades and progress reports. The athletic department had people on staff who dealt only with the academics—they monitored all our grades and if we had a problem, they'd sit down and talk with us about what we needed to do to get our grades up. They had a system in place to keep us from falling behind.

Which was good, because college was a drastic change for me, and it came as quite a shock. I had the awesome responsibility of going to class, taking notes, then trying to decipher them and then memorize them. Now, that was a fun game to participate in, but regurgitation didn't seem like the best way to learn. My college education didn't make me a more learned person as it should have—I don't think many colleges succeed in doing that very well. The teachers are underpaid and overworked. With rare exceptions, like my course in Black History, I

"His message is always the same: 'Avoid alcohol and drugs. Establish goals. Discipline yourself and achieve them.'"—Arkansas Gazette (Photo by Gary Speed, courtesy Arkansas Gazette)

wasn't challenged to think, to examine and explore ideas.

But the Black History course alone gave me something very crucial—it made a connection for me and helped give me an understanding of my heritage.

It helped me understand more about the condition of so many blacks today. The number of young teenage fathers—and mothers—is very troubling. A lot of people seem to equate having kids to being an adult. And until we change that attitude and focus on birth control, we're going to continue to have a big problem. Even when I was growing up, it was considered something to be able to brag about having fathered a child: "Yeah, she has my baby"; "yeah, I've got a couple of kids."

I never did understand that. To me, you're not a man until you're able to take care of that child. I don't want to sound like a hypocrite because when I was that age I was interested in chasing girls too—and I probably wouldn't have considered the consequences. Fortunately, basketball occupied a lot of my time, so I couldn't chase women night after night.

If you look back into history, it's not hard to understand the source of this attitude. That's not to say it's an excuse—but there is an explanation. In the structure of slavery, the black male was put in a position where he had little or no authority or influence over his family. He was valued as a work animal and as breeding stock. Add that history to the overall attitude about sex today—then it starts to seem normal, as if that's the way things should be. We have a big task ahead of us to change that attitude.

In a sense, I always felt isolated from the university. I went to class, studied and played basketball. I wasn't involved in any other activities. I didn't have time to socialize if I intended to be successful in class and on the court, so I made my choice to concentrate on those. And that is where I focused my attention for four years. I didn't think about the pros until my senior year in college. Coach mentioned the pros to me, but he didn't dwell on it. And neither did I.

But college—even though it didn't challenge me to think the way I wish it had—gave me the chance to practice discipline and learn how to work the system. I have to say that getting my college degree is the most emotionally rewarding of all my accomplishments. It's thrilling to win a game, or a championship. It's a downer to lose a big game. But the next day, all of that's over. The satisfaction of working hard and getting my degree has stayed with me. And I expect it will.

Needless to say, I never regretted my decision to go to the University of Arkansas. The fans were the best. And Eddie Sutton was the best.

Moncrief pays tribute to his wife and mother before the last home game of his college career. (Photo by Steve Keesee, courtesy Arkansas Gazette)

*F*ebruary, 1979: It is Sidney Moncrief's last home game as a Razorback, and 9,339 fans are jammed into Barnhill Arena. Many of them have come early just to watch him warm up. Everyone seems to have a camera and Barnhill seems to have been invaded by lightning bugs. It is a night brimming with emotion. Before the game begins, Sidney pulls his wife and mother from the audience and leads them to mid-court for an ovation that lasts two minutes.

The fans cheer every basket; they almost bring the house down when he intercepts a pass just before the end of the first half, scurries down the court and slam-dunks just before the buzzer. Moncrief turns and twists. He blocks. He leaps above everybody else for rebounds. He looks like a quarterback firing the ball down-court and hitting U.S. Reed in stride. He scores 29 points in the thrashing of Houston.

When he leaves the game for good the applause which has been deafening all night long grows so loud the arena vibrates. And when the fans leave Barnhill that night, they leave knowing an era has passed.

Moncrief reaches for two at Barnhill Arena. (Photo by Bill Doshier)

Moncrief on take-off. (Photo by Bill Doshier)

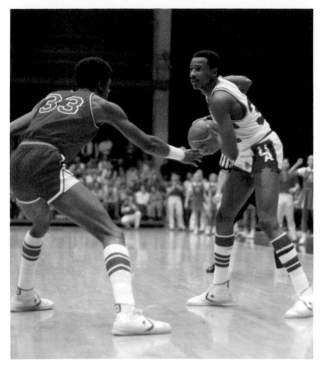

(Photo by Bill Doshier)

(Photo by Bill Doshier)

Two defenders try to stand between Moncrief and his goal.
(Photo by Bill Doshier)

Moncrief and the Hogs always packed them in at Barnhill (Photo by Bill Doshier)

(Photo by Bill Doshier)

(Photo by Bill Doshier)

(Photo by Bill Doshier)

(Photo by Bill Doshier)

CHAPTER FIVE

THE PROS

BY THE END OF MY SENIOR YEAR I WAS PRETTY certain I would be going to the pros, but it didn't matter who drafted me. I'd heard that L.A. would take Magic Johnson—so all that was left for me were cities with cold temperatures. I didn't particularly want to go to a city the size of New York or Chicago; and I knew nothing—zero—about Milwaukee, except that it was very cold.

When Milwaukee drafted me in the first round, my main thoughts were, *I'm going to get a chance very few people get,* and *I'm going to freeze to death.*

When I first arrived in Milwaukee I was afraid—not intimidated, just plain afraid. There was so much I didn't know about the professional game, about the travel, about my teammates, about the organization—or about the city, which seemed so big to me.

Junior Bridgeman and his wife, who became two of our best friends, were sort of like our own personal welcome wagon. They helped us get to know Milwaukee and feel at home there. Junior and other veterans— Harvey Catchings, Brian Winters, and Quinn Buckner—bent over backwards to help me adjust to all the newness. They were always giving me advice about what to do and what not to do—both on and off the court. When I didn't play as much—or as well—as I thought I should have, they'd have words of encouragement. They'd tell me what they knew about playing a certain opponent. But mostly they encouraged me to watch out for myself and to stand up for myself within the organization. They gave me advice on how to negotiate my contract—what to look for, what not to look for. I couldn't have been luckier with my teammates.

Sitting on the bench in the pros was a big adjustment. Back in college, Coach Sutton had talked about role playing, how certain players were starters and the job of the other players was to support the starters—and to wait for their opportunity to go in and make things happen. I had to remind myself of some of Coach Sutton's talks while sitting on the Milwaukee bench.

Wait for your opportunity and when it comes, take advantage of it, I told myself. When

Moncrief was the sixth player in the Bucks' 21-year history to have his number retired. (courtesy Milwaukee Bucks)

Moncrief defending against Chicago's David Greenwood. (courtesy Milwaukee Bucks)

Moncrief makes a near-impossible over-the-head shot against future teammate Jack Sikma of the Seattle Supersonics. (courtesy Milwaukee Bucks)

In a Milwaukee Journal poll, Moncrief was a landslide winner as the Bucks' all-time favorite player, over Kareem Abdul-Jabbar and Oscar Robertson. (courtesy Milwaukee Bucks)

Moncrief drives in for a reverse two-handed layup. Defending on the play is Alex English. (courtesy Milwaukee Bucks)

I found it especially discouraging, I had to tell myself, *Now when you were a starter at Arkansas, there were people on the bench and you knew what an important role they played for you. But now you're in that position and you can't take it, can you?* I had to give myself that lecture quite often.

The NBA brought a level of play that was a real challenge for me. I'm fairly small for the pros—and I tell you, it can get rough. There's plenty of pushing, elbow swinging and foot stomping. If that doesn't wear your body down, the traveling will. When I was on the road, I lifted weights, took steam baths for relaxation, and did some reading. When I wasn't on the road, I didn't spend a lot of time with any of the team: I tried to spend my free time with my family. Doing that rejuvenated me and helped me regroup for the next road trip.

Life in the pros is certainly not all excitement—lots of it is routine. On the morning of a game, we'd have a scouting report on the other team, hearing about its main plays and main players. At 1:00 or so I'd take a two-hour nap. At 3:30 I'd eat my pre-game meal—probably some baked fish, steamed vegetables and a salad. Now, I'm not a superstitious person, but I found if I didn't have my afternoon nap, or if I ate at 5:00 instead of 3:30—that threw my game off. I needed my schedule.

We usually arrived at the game site two hours before tipoff. When we were at home, I'd go half an hour earlier than that so I could do some shooting before anyone else was on the court or in the stands. I liked having that time alone to concentrate solely on my shooting. Then I'd go into the locker room and watch the film until time to warm up with the team.

Pro ball requires a mental toughness that's not required of a college player. The pro scouting reports are much more useful; but while I knew more about the player I was up against, he, in turn, knew more about me. So we knew about each other, but the question was, how could we put our knowledge to use on the court?

Moncrief takes a jumper in the Bucks' new home, the Bradley Center. (courtesy Milwaukee Bucks)

Moncrief blocks the sun ... a Phoenix Sun, that is. (courtesy Milwaukee Bucks)

Moncrief stuffs one against the Washington Bullets. (courtesy Milwaukee Bucks)

A lot of players will listen to scouting reports but pay very little if any attention to them. Or they'll watch a film and see a player do the same thing over and over—like always move to the right—and not do a thing to stop that move once they get on the court. One of my strengths was the ability to take what I've picked up on reports and on film and use that to my advantage on the court.

It didn't take me long to realize that I was playing for a coach with a system that made sense. Don Nelson was the person who helped me develop my pro game—which is not the same as the college game. I may have been a great college player, but that's not the same as being a great pro player. Coach Nelson taught me all I needed

to know about professional basketball, and he did it in a way that made it fun.

He made it fun by building his offense around his players instead of vice versa. And he made sure that his offensive and defensive set gave his players enough flexibility to use their own style and abilities to get the job done. For instance, there's a certain fundamental way to dribble a ball or to shoot, but if our style was different, that was all right with Coach Nelson, provided you accomplished his purpose.

We did have to work as a team—he was good about drafting and signing people who not only knew the game of basketball but who were unselfish and team oriented. And though we couldn't be prima donnas, if we

Moncrief flips in a reverse left-handed layup. Teammates in on the play are Terry Cummings (#34) and Larry Krystkowiak (#42). (courtesy Milwaukee Bucks)

Moncrief was named NBA Player of the Month in December 1981. (courtesy Milwaukee Bucks)

(courtesy Milwaukee Bucks)

*F*ive seconds remain on the score clock in the third game of the 1982 playoffs. Philadelphia—leading the series 2-0—is ahead 91-90. After a time-out, Moncrief takes the ball out of bounds and passes to Bob Lanier near the top of the key. He darts toward Lanier, takes a handoff, dribbles to within six feet of the basket. He stops, takes one of his patented leaps, and tosses the ball high above the long, stretched arms of Julius Erving. It banks through at the buzzer, and over 11,000 fans go wild with elation. Later, the fans have even more reason to marvel over Moncrief's effort when they learn that he made the winning basket with a right hand that was numb (from a collision earlier in the game) from the tips of his two smallest fingers to the wrist.

ad-libbed rather than doing a play exactly as drawn, if we deviated within the confines of the system—as long as we got the job done, that was fine with him.

Not all coaches are that way. In college our playing was very structured. When I started playing for Milwaukee, Coach Nelson was one of the few coaches in professional ball who gave players the leeway to make decisions while on the court. Furthermore, if we had an idea on how to run a play, how to set a pick, how to play defense, or how to play a player, we knew we could tell him and he would listen to us and respect what we had to say.

Once, for instance, we were playing the Chicago Bulls, and it was my assignment to guard Michael Jordan. After watching the films, Coach Nelson said, "Jordan obviously likes to drive right, so I want you to play him tight and force him to his left. Then we'll give you double-team help to the left." But I

Moncrief shows the style that made him the Bucks' career leader for free throws attempted and made. (Photo by Jeff Mitchell, courtesy Arkansas Gazette)

told Coach that I thought he could go left on his left-hand side almost as well as he could go right. "I think what we should do is give him a little more room and force him to shoot the jumper. Then if he does go left or right, I'll double with the closest guy." In this instance, Coach Nelson, who always gave serious consideration to our recommendations even if he decided against them, said, "Okay, we won't play him so close. Back off and give him the outside shot. And don't let him beat you to the bucket."

Don Nelson also has a special talent for reading a player and for knowing what it takes to motivate that player, and in return, he gained our respect. When you have a coach you respect, it makes all the difference in the world. Coach Nelson was that kind of a coach. I learned a lot about leadership from him.

When Coach Nelson went to Golden State, he was replaced by Del Harris, his assistant. Del Harris knows as much about the technical aspects of the game as any coach, and more than most. He does his homework and spends a lot of time watching film and analyzing players. Like Coach Nelson, he was open to our recommendations, and he was fairly sensitive to some of the pressures of being an NBA player.

Say, for instance, that we had played four games in six days and lost all of them. We have another game coming up in two days. Now, do you practice the guys because you've lost the last four games and need two days of practice to win the next one? Or do you say, "Maybe they're tired of basketball and of seeing me. Maybe they just need a day off to get away from it"?

Some coaches, because they never played pro basketball, or any basketball period, do the former, and all you do with an attitude like that is alienate players who *are* tired and need a day off. To his credit, Coach Harris, like Coach Nelson, was more likely to give us a day off. He would come up to me, or Paul Pressey, or Jack Sikma and say, "What do you think?" And of course we'd say we needed the day off.

Coach Harris knows that in the pros, just like in any business, employees are not going to be fully productive if they don't feel they have a say in what is going on.

My fear of being in the pros soon dissipated. It helped that I was never in awe of the talent of the big-name players—such as Larry Bird, Michael Jordan and Dr J. I respected the stars and their talent, but I also knew I could compete.

Playing the best challenged me to be my best—to test my limits. It was also just plain fun to play against players with such skill. I found I could be playing very hard against a guy on another team and still be impressed with his play. If an opponent made a good shot or a great move or an impressive pass, in my mind I'd say, *What a play!* Sometimes I even complimented the player if I got the chance. I think you can play better if you

allow yourself to respect your opponent.

I played against so many good players that it's impossible, really, to single out the best. Of course, Larry Bird would have to be high on anybody's list. He's intense, he works hard, he's versatile, and he's a real team player. With our difference in size I didn't guard Larry that much in the pros. I did go one-on-one with him the last game of my college career.

No matter how great a college coach is, he doesn't have the time or the expertise to fully analyze an opponent. So when I played Bird in college, we didn't have any detailed tendency reports on him. When I guarded him the second half of the game, I had no idea of his specific moves. I had not seen him play before, and I was too busy the first half guarding someone else to watch him. I was simply playing defense the way I had always played it. His offensive skills were not nearly

The 1985-86 Bucks. Moncrief is fourth from left, bottom row. (courtesy Milwaukee Bucks)

as refined as they are now, and he didn't have teammates who could get the ball to him like he does now, so my athletic ability allowed me to do a pretty good job on him. Sometimes I guarded Larry in the pros, but it was a different story then. I couldn't really play him in the pros—I'm too small.

If I were bigger and could play him, though, I'd push him to his right, because he likes to move to his left to shoot. I'd push him to his right, play him tight to force him to drive, and then I'd try to block him out on any shots. On post, I'd try to front him and not let him get the basketball.

What can I say about Magic Johnson except that he deserves his name? He controls the tempo of the game. He gets all the players involved and, like Bird, he plays an unselfish ball game. He's very right-handed, so he has a strong tendency to move to his right. Even though he's good enough to go left or right, you play him to go right. His outside shot is pretty good too, so you have to play him tight. If he's on the post, he's very difficult to guard because he's so big—he's 6'8"—and agile. You can't play behind him; if he gets the ball with his back to the basket, he's just going to hook it. You can't front him; he'll be able to catch a lob.

What you do with Magic is pick him up in the back court and make him turn. You don't want him coming at you face forward; you want him to come at you with his back turned and back you down the court. That way you can get help from your defense. Magic is not as difficult to keep from scoring as Jordan or Bird. But he's such a great all-around player, and like Bird, he can beat you so many different ways. If he can't beat you scoring, he'll beat you with his passing, and his play-making—he'll beat you by making things happen on the court.

Dr. J was extremely difficult to guard. He is big. And he is good. Doc is right-handed and he likes his right. But if he wanted to shoot a jump shot, he liked to move to his left, take one dribble,

then pull up and bank it off the glass. With Doc, I tried to take away his right hand and force him to take the jumper. On the post, you couldn't front him, you couldn't play behind him—you had to play him in-between. I used a move Eddie Sutton had taught me in college (we called it half-mooning): face him from the side and get a hand in front of his face. You also had to try to keep Doc out of the open court—he was one of the best open-court players in the history of the sport—by picking him up early and not letting him get the basketball.

Mostly, though, with Dr. J, you just had to yell for help.

Most of my colleagues and opponents were good sports as well as good players. I don't remember if any coach ever threw around the word "sportsmanship" to me. But I knew it was important, even if they didn't preach it all the time. If someone on our team did something unsportsmanlike, the coach let the players know that was not the thing to do. In some programs, unsportsmanlike conduct is encouraged. But I can't think of any team I played on where it was. And being around those type coaches certainly molded my sense of sportsmanship.

That's not to say I haven't been in fights on the court. My fights were usually provoked by rough play. If I felt someone was being unsportsmanlike to me on a consistent basis, well, I'm not the type of person who can give, give, give, give.

Maybe it's because I spent so much time on the streets back in the projects, but my stopping point is fairly quick on the basketball court. I wouldn't do anything to hurt anyone intentionally, but I'm not going to let anyone intimidate me or put Sidney in a position where he can injure himself.

If a player is pushed too far, he becomes intimidated in his play. If someone beats on me for the entire ball game and I sit and take it, then I might as well be sitting on the bench because I won't be able to help my team if I am that intimidated. If someone pushes me to a certain level—well, I have been known to strike back.

It happened in college and it happened in the pros. Once we were playing Texas A&M in Fayetteville. At that time A&M had a reputation for being rough and dirty and for taking the game away from you largely by intimidation. That night, they were pretty much living up to their reputation, especially Rynn Wright and Jarvis Williams, who were strong and very athletic and determined to intimidate anyone that got near them. It got to the point in the game where Jarvis, I think it was, actually elbowed me in the stomach. It was not an accident; it was not in the course of a play. He was guarding someone else and in passing by me, he simply did it. I didn't appreciate that, and I lost my temper. At that point, I was no longer on the basketball court; I was in the streets—and I went after him with a vengence. Well, that pretty much cleared the benches, and it became quite a brawl. As I recall, when the dust settled and we resumed play, we played quite well. They didn't try to intimidate us anymore.

But fighting is still wrong. I tell kids the fact I got into a fight doesn't make it right; it's still wrong and I made a mistake.

I'm not proud of my fights. Sometimes, in the course of a game, I wish I could take my emotions out of my life and say, "Go away and don't intervene with what's happening here." But I couldn't always do that—especially in the pros, where everything is so competitive and where intimidation gets to be a part of the game.

Occasionally, Moncrief felt obliged to let the refs know they goofed. (Photo by Gary Speed, courtesy Arkansas Gazette)

Once when we were playing Detroit, Bill Laimbeer elbowed me a couple of times going down the court. On the very next play, I elbowed him and he flopped like I'd hit him hard. And I hadn't. I was kicked out of the game and fined for elbowing—which I deserved.

I've also had technical fouls called. If I thought an official made a bad call, I let him know. If he made a good call, I'd tell him that too. I'm talking about pro ball now. It's a job. I'm getting paid for it, so I think it's okay to let the official know when he's made a big goof. In fact, we have to keep pressure on them to do their job right.

The nature of the pro game demands that players be more aggressive. Some games get extemely rough. Lots of people ask me how it was to play Detroit. The bad boys are certainly more aggressive than most teams. That's why they win ball games. I respect them for it—except when they cross the line between aggressive and dirty. Occasionally they do cross that line, and sometimes they cross it intentionally. But for the most part, they are more aggressive than dirty.

I don't want to excuse professional players when we exhibit bad sportsmanship, because we obviously have not always been a good example. But I'd challenge the theory that the worst examples of bad sportsman- ship come from the pros. There, at least, the official recognizes he is dealing with professionals—that this is what the players do for a living.

I've never seen professional players argue with officials like they do in college. Junior-high, high-school and college coaches—they should absolutely not allow players to belittle an official or make a scene on the basketball court. Such behavior should be taboo.

There's no one team in the pros that I dreaded playing, and there's no one team that I looked forward to playing more than the others. All of the teams are good now. It wasn't that way several years ago. Then we knew who we had to really gear up to play, and the other forty percent of the time we could just about show up and win.

Not so today. True, five or six teams are the cream of the crop in a given year, but even the lesser teams can beat you, so I learned to focus and be ready to play each team.

People ask me what change I'd like to see in the pro rules. The answer is—not much. The game is rough, but from what I hear, the game was rougher fifteen years ago than it is now. I heard there were more fights then, but the games weren't televised as much so there wasn't as much publicity. Hand-checking was legal, so it was a lot more aggressive.

I don't think a zone defense should be allowed. It would slow the game down too much and take away the one-on-one aspect of defense that's so exciting to play and to watch.

I think the bucket is the right height. Dunking is here to stay, and so is the three-point rule—it's the best thing that's happened to basketball. From a psychological standpoint a three-pointer can be devastating to the opponents.

I had my share of success in the pros. And my share of excitement. Making the All-Star team was especially exciting the first time, but you can't establish the teamwork and rapport that is important to me in one game like that.

I remember getting my first paycheck, which was a substantial sum of money— thousands of dollars. I walked around with it in my pocket thinking, "I'm not poor anymore." That's a great feeling. The down side of having so much is that once a person ceases to be poor, he doesn't understand what it is to be poor. I can say, "I know what it's like to be poor." I can take you by the projects and say, "I used to live here—I know what they are going through." But I don't. The minute I had that first paycheck, it became harder for me to remember what being poor was like. That's why there's such a gap of understanding in our country.

I got along fine with the organization. I

Moncrief quickly overcame his fear of professional competition. (courtesy Milwaukee Bucks)

never looked upon my relationship with the owners as being owned by them but as working for them. I contracted with the owners to play basketball, and yes, they controlled my basketball life from October to June. But my summers, and my soul, were my own.

A player has to decide how much he is going to let the organization control his life off the court. I didn't particularly enjoy a lot of things we were required to do, but I was never put in a situation that I felt I had to refuse—from a moral, ethical, or religious standpoint. If I had found myself in such a situation, then I would not have done it.

Some things I simply would not have done. I would not, for example, be a part of a beer commercial. It bothers me that alcohol is so glamourized and so connected with sports through television commercials. Even though the NBA is the forerunner of the Just Say No movement—we counsel young people about the problems of alcohol and drug abuse— probably 75 percent of our sponsorship money comes from beer and tobacco. If you watch an NBA game, you'll see plenty of beer commercials—with NBA players in them as well.

I understand and support freedom of speech. At least a person watching television has the option of not watching the commercial. But people who go to the game can't watch it without seeing the courtside advertising—which is largely for alcohol and cigarettes. I'd like to see those billboards banned, because they have a captive audience. These are drugs, and I don't like seeing them associated with sports.

(True, there are people in sports who do drugs. But I can tell you there are plenty of people who don't. Sure, I could have found drugs easily enough if I had hung out at certain places, but I can honestly tell you that I never saw drugs in the locker room in all the time I played pro ball.)

Ultimately, though, each of us has to decide whether to abide by the decrees of the owners, or whether to say no and face the consequences. Those dilemmas exist in any business, and in any job—not just in sports.

Making the right decision in those situations is part of facing life head on.

CHAPTER SIX

THE FUTURE

IN THE SUMMER OF '89, I HAD TO FACE ANOTHER decision—whether or not to retire. I had always said three things would determine when I was going to retire. First and foremost: when I no longer enjoyed the game and the life that went with it—when I could't take the travel, when I couldn't deal with management, when I couldn't deal with teammates, when I just couldn't motivate myself to prepare over the summer to play basketball.

Number two: when nobody wanted me—of course.

And number three: when the money wasn't there, when I didn't feel that I was being paid enough to do what I do. As long as someone was willing to pay me handsomely for doing what I enjoy, I wasn't going to leave clean, honest money lying on the table.

I was no longer getting in as much playing time as I used to, because I was not the player I had been five years earlier. My body was in good condition, and I was a smarter player; but I was older, and I couldn't compete for 30 to 45 minutes like I once did. I played better if I played 20 to 28 minutes a game. Sure, I *wanted* to play longer. I wanted to be in the game all the time—that was my ego talking. But common sense said, *You can't, you wouldn't be as effective playing all the time.*

Sidney Moncrief was the first to put his print on the Celebrity Sidewalk created by Little Rock Unlimited Progress. (courtesy Mrs. Bernice Perkins)

Sidney and Debra Moncrief in Central Park. (courtesy Arkansas Democrat)

Still, sitting on the bench could be frustrating. I had sat on the bench for years in junior high, but then, the person out there on the court was better than I was. In the NBA, the person out there was also often better, but he might not be the best person to have out there for the benefit of the team.

On the first of July, 1989, my contract expired with Milwaukee and I became a free agent. No one knocked down my door to sign me. I could have chosen not to retire, and I'm sure by January or February someone would have gone down with an injury and a call would have come.

But after playing for ten years, I didn't want my life, or the tone of my life, decided by someone else. And I wasn't sure I was still totally comitted to giving it my all, that at mid-year I wouldn't say, "I don't need this, I'm tired and I'm going to retire."

At first I worked out on the track and on the court and worked hard. But as the days went by and no one called, I had trouble getting motivated to go out there and train, just to be able to prove to people that I could still play. I realized I no longer felt I had anything to prove.

In a way, I tossed retirement about in the back of my mind all summer. I'd be working out and I'd find myself saying,

"What am I doing this for? I don't want to play anymore. My knees can't take it. My back can't take it. Mentally I can't do it anymore." Then the next week I'd find myself saying, "I'm going to keep playing. I really like doing this."

I tend to act impulsively, and I made the decision rather suddenly. I had reached the point when all three factors kicked in. When I realized that, believe me, it was not a difficult decision to make. I made it. And I like my decision. Ten years of being told what to do—even though I was very well paid and well treated—ten years of being controlled by a schedule and by management—was enough.

The decision was not traumatic because I had never considered pro basketball my life. I considered it *part* of my life. Yes, I worked hard at it, and yes, I enjoyed it—but it wasn't as much fun for me as it had been

when I was in junior high, or high school, or even in college. After all, we were a bunch of grown men out there throwing a ball around. What we were doing was not really serious. Being a heart surgeon is serious, being an engineer is serious, designing hospitals is serious, teaching kids is serious, having the skill to repair an automobile is serious. Playing basketball is entertainment—pure and simple.

People ask me if I would ever consider coaching. Actually, if I hadn't made the pros I probably would have ended up coaching at a high school. But at this time, I would not want to coach junior high, or high school—or even college. In those situations a coach has to deal with too many factors—the students, alumni, parents, faculty, assistant coaches, administrations, athletic department, media and fans. That's more than I would want to take on. If I coached, I'd want to coach at the pro level. There, the coach deals with the

"Sidney Moncrief was the greatest player, the greatest human being I ever coached."—Don Nelson (Photo by John D. Simmons, courtesy Arkansas Democrat)

players, the front office, and the fans. He doesn't have to be all things to all people, so he can concentrate much more on the game of basketball.

I'm not looking for a coaching job in the pros, but if an opportunity came my way, I would consider it. I still love the game, and I like the comfortable but simple lifestyle it afforded me. It afforded me time to give to my business, time to give to service groups and time for us to do the things we like to do. Debra and I enjoy traveling, movies, playing tennis … I play tennis more than any other sport. I play at golf, but more than nine holes gets too long for me.

There will probably come a time when I miss basketball more than I do now. I watch games and it doesn't pain me. I watch them as a fan—as a fairly critical fan, but as a fan.

I never did learn to like the cold, but I did like the people of Milwaukee, and I miss them. I'll always remember them as warm and supportive. I hope when they remember me, they'll say that I was dedicated, that when I put my foot on that court I gave everything I had to give. I hope all my fans from all of my basketball careers had half the pleasure watching me play as I had in playing.

But for now, I'm not thinking about coaching pros—I'm thinking about the path I've chosen and I'm happy with that.

One benefit of retirement is getting to spend more time with Debra and Jon Phillip, our son. He is just learning to talk and every day he learns something new—and every day I learn something new. I'm realizing even more how much children model themselves after adults. Not long after he learned to walk, he put on my hat, said "Bye" and started toward the door—obviously imitating me. I'm very fortunate to have this much time to spend with him; many parents have no choice about the hours they have to be away from their children. I didn't realize until now how much they are missing, or how much I was missing.

I own a car dealership in Little Rock.

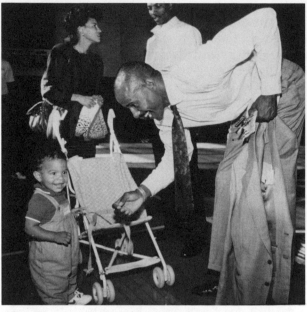

After announcing his retirement, Moncrief shares a moment with his son, Jon Phillip, as Debra stands nearby. (Photo by John Sykes, courtesy Arkansas Democrat)

People also ask me why I chose the particular business I did. I'm certainly not one with great mechanical knowledge, but I always liked cars. I knew that I needed to buy a small company and have it operating by the time I retired. I wanted a business that had the potential for a good return on my investment and one which paid me a decent salary. I wanted a product that would appeal to people and one that had a customer base. Our dealership has five profit centers: new and used sales, parts, service, and finance and insurance—so there's a bit of a hedge if one of the areas isn't performing too well.

I chose this particular manufacturer— General Motors—because it produces a fine product. I really am enjoying the challenge of owning my own business and making decisions that will shape the future of my company. We sell a good product. We stand behind our product and our word. It's never boring. It involves people—and that's important to me. It's frustrating to see an unhappy sales or service customer, but it's very gratifying to make that person happy. In my business, as in my life, I want to learn from my mistakes and correct them.

I'm happy with another path I've chosen—a spiritual path. Like I've mentioned earlier, I was forced to go to church as a child and the teaching I got there helped give me a grounding in right and wrong. But only in the last couple of years have I realized the spiritual connection in my life.

I was so caught up with going to college, being an NBA player, trying to compete, and trying to make more money that I was distracted. But I always had the time—I just didn't take it—to take a good look at, my spiritual self. The old saying that you don't get spiritual until you get in trouble is probably all too often true. I spent my entire career in succeeding, in doing well, in prospering, and in making more money.

You can easily get to a point where you don't think spiritual well-being is important. But it is.

Nothing particular happened to cause me to soul search. It was just time—time, and Debra. Debra's a very strong woman, and she has a religious commitment which helps in our relationship—and in our lives. Her spiritual strength has helped me to be a stronger person. It's led me to *want* to be a better Christian.

Now that I've retired from basketball, what do I see for my future? I want to devote more time to the public sector. My philosophy is never say never, but I don't see myself going into politics—I don't see myself as a politician. I'm a doer—I see what

Moncrief shares a laugh with friends Geese Ausbie and Darrell Walker. (Photo by Kelly Quinn, courtesy Arkansas Gazette)

has to be done and I do it. A politician has to play so many little side games just to get a task done. I'm not comfortable playing those games, even though I can see that it is sometimes important to what has to be done down the line.

I chose to go into business in Arkansas because I was raised in Arkansas, because I love Arkansas, and because I still feel the potential is there for great things to happen. But it's going to take a lot of education, and a lot of work.

As far as race relations are concerned, Arkansas is probably as good a place as any to raise Jon Phillip. I'm more sensitive to the problems here because it's my home, but the problems of race are no worse here than anywhere else in our country. I'm used to having people look at me as though I don't belong. I run into that everywhere I go: New York, Boston, Hawaii, Dallas—everywhere. Just last week I was in Florida at an expensive hotel and people were giving me that look. I don't see that raising my son in Arkansas is a disadvantage as far as race is concerned. I do see it as a disadvantage as far as education is concerned.

We have a big problem with education in Arkansas, and there's no simple solution for it. We need a strong academic system, obviously; our colleges need to be well-financed and they need to provide a strong academic education. And of course we need good basic education for everyone.

The Triplets—Ron Brewer, Sidney Moncrief, and Marvin Delph—return to Little Rock for a charity benefit in 1988. (Photo by Kelly Quinn, courtesy Arkansas Gazette)

But when we talk education, we always seem to talk about the college degree, when the fact is, not everybody should be channeled into college. We simply must have a well-trained, skilled, and productive work force. We need to put much more focus on job-training skills. I don't think that we've done a good job of taking the resources we have in Arkansas and developing them. It looks good to talk about getting industry to move here from out of state, but what are they moving to? A work force that is not trained and an academic system that is below par.

We can't do what we need to do without more money—and smart use of the money. I don't know how we can convince the people here that we have to make a big investment in education—basic, technical, and academic. Arkansas, like most of America, has a "no more taxes" mentality, and it's hard to change that mentality. But we aren't going to have much of a future unless we are willing to sacrifice for it.

Education aside, I intend to spend more time with community and youth services. I hope I can help convince kids that grew up the way I did that they can make it. I hope I can be a part of helping them have some hope, some goals to work toward.

When I was junior-high age, I had no goals. If a teacher had asked me then to write about how I saw myself ten or twenty years down the road, I don't know what I would have said, because—and this is the sad part about how I grew up—I didn't see much of a future. Until I started Scouting, I didn't have any role models. I wasn't part of any activities where I could see someone doing something positive and say, "I'd like to be like that." I didn't realize then that by not setting goals, I was making choices every day that set me in the direction I would go.

I was lucky that Boy Scouts and the community club were there when I was a bit older. I was lucky Dave Shaeffer, and Coach Ripley, and Coach Elders were there. They helped keep me out of trouble and nudged me toward having a goal. That goal—to be a coach—led me to work to get into college.

And even though I'm not a coach, having a goal kept me going in a positive direction.

Some of my friends never headed in that positive direction. They continued making decisions that made them open game for criminal court. Some of my friends are still in prison today. I could have been there too if I hadn't decided that there were choices to be made, and ultimately, I had to be the one to make them.

That's the point I try to get across to young people when I talk with them. I don't think it helps to lecture to them—so I don't. I just tell them that they have choices to make. I ask them to set a goal of getting better at something they like to do—something that will not harm them. I tell them one of the most important things I've learned, which is: success is not given to you. You have to work for it. If you're born in difficult circumstances, you have to work harder. But you can make it if you set your mind to it. Believe me, I didn't wake up one morning knowing how to play basketball—it took years and years of hard work. And it's taking hard work to learn how to run a business. And it's hard work to be a parent. I don't kid myself that in talking to young people I'm making a world of difference in anyone's life. I'm afraid talks don't change attitudes for a long period of time. But if I can plant one good idea into one kid's head, or if I can nudge one kid toward making good choices about his or her life, then that's a start.